ANCHOR BOOKS

LOADS OF LAUGHS

Edited by

Heather Killingray

First published in Great Britain in 1997 by
ANCHOR BOOKS
1-2 Wainman Road, Woodston,
Peterborough, PE2 7BU
Telephone (01733) 230761

HB ISBN 1 85930 479 6
SB ISBN 1 85930 474 5

FOREWORD

Anchor Books is a small press, established in 1992, with the aim of promoting readable poetry to as wide an audience as possible.

We hope to establish an outlet for writers of poetry who may have struggled to see their work in print.

The poems presented here have been selected from many entries. Editing proved to be a difficult task and as the Editor, the final selection was mine.

What makes you laugh? Is it your favourite celebrity, perhaps a friend or relative. Whether a situation comedy or a clown at a circus everyone has a chuckle now and again. Poets in this collection have a variety of verse to make us laugh. I'm sure a page of this a day is the best tonic, everyone needs, 'laughter being the best medicine'.

So keep those frowns at bay, this book at hand and escape life's monotony.

I trust this selection will delight and please the authors and all those who enjoy reading poetry.

Heather Killingray
Editor

CONTENTS

AMERICAN BREAKFAST

To order breakfast in the States
Can easily delay and make you late.
Nothing's easy, nothing's simple!
Let me give you an example.

'Hi-ya guys! How-ya doing?
Nice to see yous all this mornin'.
Can I get you folks some juice?
Anything you care to choose?
Orange, apple or blueberry drink?
Grapefruit! OK, white or pink?

What are you guys going to eat?
Toast? - Will that be rye or wheat?
Eggs? - Easy over or sunny side up?
Can I fill your coffee cups?
Decaff or regular? White or black?
Cream and sugar in the rack.

What? You're going? No time to stay?
OK guys - then *have a nice day!*'

Anne Crofton Dearle

I HATE WINTER

If I could choose the season
When it comes my time to go,
I'd make it in the autumn
Before the fall of snow,
Though days are so much shorter,
Leaves still crown the trees,
And old folk in the bus queues
Don't stamp their feet and freeze.
In winter, no-one listens,
However much they moan,
And still the wind bites deeper,
Sometimes to chill the bone;
Spring is so long in coming,
And the waiting's tedious too,
So I'd take my leave in autumn,
If that's alright with you?

I've always hated winter,
With its fog, and ice and snow,
So I'd never even miss it,
In that, 'Hot spot', down below!

Sam Stafford

THE LAUGH

Laughter makes the world go round,
It's a most enjoyable sound.
Starting low inside your tummy,
It can burst out, when things are funny.
Sometimes it escapes as only a titter,
But can become a full blown laugh,
So please don't go round feeling bitter,
Go on, try it, it's a blast.

Sandra Houghton

THE LITTLE BOOKWORM

You are a little bookworm,
I've seen you, once before.
Cos you live here, in the library,
Behind the sliding door.

I've seen you read the best of them,
A swot of some dimension.
And you don't seem to worry much,
When a certain subject, needs attention.

I've heard you laugh, outrageously,
At some verse you've found inspiring.
But you've cried your little eyes out,
When it's turned all sad, and with no style - in.

So here I am, in fighting form,
With this know-it-all forever.
But I'm so glad that you're my friend.
Cos I think, you're rather clever.

Sue Williams

PERSONAL PROFILE

Some people call me slapper,
Because I've lost my hair,
Whilst others call me three chins,
With several more to spare,
Some people call me no neck,
Because my head's too big,
Whilst others call me carpet,
Because I wear a wig,
Some people call me Bugsy,
Because my teeth protrude,
Whilst others call me crater,
For looking like the moon,
Some people call me satellite,
My ears just like a dish,
Whilst others call me gilly,
For breathing like a fish,
Some people call me Donald,
For walking like a duck,
Whilst others call me five waists,
Despite my tummy tuck,
Some people call me toady,
Because of bulging eyes,
Whilst others call me Nelly,
Because of jumbo thighs,
Some people call me lofty,
Because I'm twelve foot three,
I bet you'd rather be yourself,
Than be a man like me!

Christopher Noon

THE VICAR GOES SWIMMING

A jolly old vicar from Bude,
Decided to swim in the nude.
A crab nipped his toe,
He shouted 'Let go'
And more that was really quite rude!

Heather Middleton

BEWARE!

The other day I boarded the stage coach bus.
At the end of my short journey I dismounted,
Tripped and fell flat on my face.
I regained the perpendicular,
Only to be assailed by the visual warning
Mind the step.
I silenced my expletive.

Ken Round

MR NOBODY

I know a man Mr Nobody
Was his name
Eating children
Was his game
He liked boys
With mustard
And girls with custard.

The next night
He dressed up bright
In the evening light
It was a wonderful sight
He tried to eat me
So I ran away
When I woke up
I said

'Phew
It was all a dream!'

Naila Hanif (13)

HEY DIDDLE DIDDLE

Once upon a starry night
While gazing at the moon
I soon did spy, when I blinked my eye
A dish running off with a spoon

Hey diddle diddle
I thought here's a riddle
A cow jumped over the moon
Just wait for a while, said the cat with a smile
And I'll tickle the dog with a broom.

Evelyn Roxburgh

FUNNY OR WHAT?

It's nice and peaceful where I'm at,
I must be dead, so that is that,
Floating upwards in my brain,
Please don't bring me back again.

Gliding through a starlit night,
Now I've passed into the light,
Glowing friends they point the way,
This must be the place I stay.

I've never been here before,
Standing at this pearly door,
Did they really let me in?
Was I washed from all my sin?

Suddenly pulled back in time,
Into a body, oh God it's mine!
I hear myself give out a groan,
Smiling doctor said welcome home.

Christine Shannon

DEAR ALICE . . .

And so you say you're getting wed again
well this really must be said,
'cause judging by your past records
the groom will soon be dead!

Of all the men you've wed before
well none did run astray.
They just sorta curled their toes up
then quietly passed away.

So now you've got to ask yourself,
did you do something wrong.
Was it something in your cooking
or was the tea a bit too strong!

So get him to the church
don't leave him in the lurch.
While we keep our fingers crossed
that he won't start turning blue,
before you say 'I do.'

And when the wedding's over
you'd best produce a will,
for once he's got it signed
you can start to lace his wine.

Don't worry about the honeymoon,
as there's only this I've left unsaid;
'By the time you've packed the suitcases
the old man will be dead!'

Pauline Johnston

THE DUST MITE'S TALE

Some dust mites lie there undisturbed,
such as on the surface where you type.
Some are crushed by a polishing cloth,
or sucked up a ruthless vacuum pipe.

Some float on the air without a care,
though brief our life and short our tour.
Yet some are trapped into a holiday.
To Ibiza and back I went I'm sure.

It was so dark for the whole long day,
with droning momentum going on forever.
But eventually the trunk was flung wide open,
and I rose in the heat like an unseen feather.

Then flicked by a towel from a bathroom rail,
I wafted down onto an envelope.
Inside I slid and was sealed for the mail,
to be delivered back home on a sliver of soap.

David Derbyshire

THE WAYS OF LAUGHTER . . .

Laughter and its cousins: smile,
Giggle, grin and smirk,
Are strictly for humans; animals
Are not so daft . . . always except
The Cheshire Cat.
Dogs know better, show their pleasure
When their ears go flat.

Olympic gods' Homeric laughter
Mocked poor mortals' bitter plight,
Laughter is cruel, think of bullies;
And remember vicarious fear,
The laughter in the cinema
In 'All quiet on the Western Front'
To see machine guns killing tommies
Cackling laughter, hard to bear;
The shark grin of a politician
Is little better than 'Say cheese'
A wedding group's smile to please.

The Chinese laughing Buddha shakes
With silent laughter and timeless joy;
We laugh to face eternity
In music, heart alone can bear
So little, must laugh and shed a tear.

As medicine, it should relax
Tension and heal . . . but often may
Be vacuous from emptiest mind,
The buffoon and the idiot's way . . .
So let us grimly scowl and snarl
Grimace if better so to do,
But laugh in pleasure when another
Will laugh with you . . .

Austin Cooper

A SMILE SHARED

A giggle a day, keeps the doctor away.
The only true words ever said.
A laugh, a giggle, a happy smile.
Cheers up the mind and the people around.
A smile is so free to give.
Costs nothing to do.
A smile that can make a person's day.
A laugh shared between two friends.
A giggle across a classroom.
Laughter to wake you up.
A laugh, a giggle, a smile to brighten ones darkest day.
How many days go around with no laughter?
How many days are full of tears.
A smile costs nothing to give.
A smile can help people live.

Paula Doyle

CRAZY ALPHABET

A's in apple, B is a word
C, it's for cockroach and D ends absurd.
E's for effect and F for a fact,
G is for Yankee and H can be hacked.
I's in a needle and J is a bird,
K can be knocked out and L's just occurred.
M is for moping, N is for nought,
O for the same thing, while P goes to port.
Q can be querulous, R's sometimes rolled,
S is a sibilant, T can be told.
U's underneath, V's on the verge
And W wonders: Is X in the purge?
Y is for asking and youth needs it too,
And Z can't do better than stay in the zoo.

Clare Meadmore

PASSIVE SHOPPING

I well recall, when I was small
I did the family shopping.
From shop to stall, you'd see me crawl
Till my wee legs were dropping.

In bakery and grocery
I'd queue for hour on hour.
My knees were saying 'No, siree.'
My feet were losing power.

At last, as I'm about to flop
I call in at the butcher.
The final stop - the corner shop.
Is this to be my future?

But now, my working days are past
It's shopping time once more.
The world is moving twice as fast.
We've superstores galore.

I whizz along from aisle to aisle
And stack my wayward trolley.
The check-out girl cracks not a smile.
Why all the melancholy?

My legs no longer take the strain.
I take the car and park it.
If I'd it all to do again
Give *me* the supermarket!

Ray Dunn

OH JOSEPHENE

Oh Josephene please
why be such a tease

Come down
From your horse
and let's play

Then I'll promise
to be good

When we stroll
through the woods

Looking for nuts
next May

A Marshall

MISSION - MISS SMITH

No misunderstandings, please.
Make no mistake, Miss Smith,
A miss is better than a mile,
More potent than a myth.

Mishap and misadventure
Were always naughty dames,
Misheard was saying something,
I misremember names.

How wrong is misinterpret,
Miscellany how fat,
Misnomer's misbegotten
And misprint can't mean that!

Then, mismanagement, farewell.
Wild misbehaviour, go!
For the missing truth, Miss Smith,
Is that I miss you so.

I hope you don't misjudge me,
I'm no misogynist.
Miss Smith, don't miss our moment,
The moment to be kissed.

Robin Brumby

A Tribute To Marti

A funny girl once passed our way,
But didn't have much time, to stay,
A Sheffield girl, a crazy lass,
Who filled our lives, with happiness.

No-one was safe, among the folk
Who gathered round, to hear her jokes,
As Marti saw the chance to pounce
Upon the unsuspecting crowd.

This slim and pretty Yorkshire girl
Brought joy and laughter, to our world;
The Queen of Satire, reigning from
Her castle, in a Yorkshire club.

We never once saw Marti cry.
Or heard her moan, or whine, or gripe,
Whilst fighting with the enemy:
The ghastly curse. The fatal C.

But now we know that Heaven is full
Of wit, and humour, joy and fun:
With a funny angel telling jokes,
About her stay,
With the Yorkshire folk!

Sandra Wolfe

PLEASURE OF SUFFERANCE

To learn how to dance
Oh my what a treat
Until I discovered he'd
Got two left feet
We got into such tangles
and tempers got frayed
He crunched up my toes
as beautiful music played
The smile on his face
as he tramps round the floor
The excruciating pain on my face
He does choose to ignore
he thinks he is wonderful
and tells everyone
If they come round to our house
He'll soon bring them on!
I just can't tell him otherwise
His ego I'd crush
I'll have to keep suffering
This adorable *mush*

Jean Smith

THE WHALE

One day when I was swimming in the briny blue,
A whale it came and ate me,
I didn't know what to do.
I thought - I know how to cure the situation.
So I curled up tight into a ball and gave it constipation!
The tension well it mounted, then with a thunderous crack,
I felt a kind of gas build up and I shot right to the back.
The whale was affronted,
Me, I was quite brave,
Now I'm an expert surfer,
Because it made a tidal wave.

Fiona McNab

SAINT NELLIE DREAD
(The Bag Lady)

. . . Yes I remember old Nellie Dread
She had fuzzy knotted hair and wore a scarf on her head

-Sling back wellies with little peek toes
She wore rings in her ears and one in her nose
With twinkling eyes Nellie plodded on cool
Claimed she often went to church, but had never gone to school

Someone offered to give her a comb and a brush
She said hold on a minute what's all the rush
My hair ain't been combed for o'er twenty year
I ain't starting now 'ave no fear

Nellie was rough, but never a bore
Did what she pleased, without breaking the law
Wore raggy old clothes tied up with string
Though she might have been odd she did her own thing

Nellie was kind to animals, loving to kids
The lah di dah folk would flip their lids
Yelling clear off you old bag, they had no tact
Up yours replied Nellie, you all put on an act

Walking the street she picked things from the floor
Whatever they were I was never quite sure
Get on with your business she shouted out loud
Nellie as usual attracted a crowd

There were thousands at the funeral the day after she died
If Nellie was looking down, she would have laughed until she cried
Flashy limousines amongst the elite
Who would have thought she used to walk down our street

It seemed Nellie was a millionaire who could not stand money
Some of our neighbours turned quite pale and funny
She might have been odd and her ideas quaint
But to my way of thinking *old Nellie Dread was a saint.*

Honora Lowther

THE WAITING GAME

Feeling quite poorly, I've got a bad toe,
So off to the Dr's I think I should go.
Into the waiting room, please take a seat,
And you really don't know who next you will meet.
Hello Mrs Brown, we all call her Peg,
Because of the fact she's got a bad leg.
She'll chatter away you can be sure about that,
Poor old dear, she fell over the cat.
That dear little boy has measles for sure,
If I should catch it is there a cure.
Was that my name they called? I don't think so,
Cos I only got here a short time ago.
Pick up a book and try for a read,
Gracious, I really must be going to seed.
I'm no use on a yacht, or as a computer boss.
So all of these books are to me a dead loss.
Let's look at the fish tank, let's take a peek,
That's no good either, they will send me to sleep.
Many people I've talked to, many friends I have met,
What did I come for? I almost forget.
I just don't believe it they have called my name,
Then two of us got up with names just the same.
Into the Dr's after a 1½ hour wait,
Please look at my toe, I can't get it straight.
Nothing much wrong there Dr retorts,
You are just feeling low and a bit out of sorts.
For the very long wait not much to show,
But in a few weeks time again I will go.
For the entertainment alone made it worthwhile
To forget all your troubles and come home with a smile.

Frances Cook

DEFINING LAUGHTER

Healthwise laughter is the tonic
To quickly expel melancholic,
To start a truce in many a fight.
Comics use it their audiences to delight.
Laughter can also be very cruel
By mimicking antics of some poor fool
Or giving verbal sarcastic replies
To remarks made by the not so wise.

E Ballard

WHY MONA HAS A SMIRK ON HER LIPS

He hardly speaks to me some days,
A passion of movement behind the canvas.
So as I sit I have the time to think.
Why I never see him embrace,
The other models or women of the town.
He could give such pleasure to us all.

I happily married to a merchant,
Consider this great beauty of an artist.
Instead of sitting me at a distance
He could have me close.
Instead of painting me
He could draw me near.

I can't help but smile
Even though his instructions are to pose as a serious woman.
Leonardo wouldn't look many times at me,
If I wasn't the model Mona Lisa.
For in the portrait of his life,
The perfect model would be a man.

Oh well, I can think, I can dream . . .

Lee Ryder

NEW YEAR

Clocks strike 12.
'Hooray the New Year.'
Now pass the wine,
Get your hands off my beer.

Starting afresh,
Though how can you be,
With your head down the loo,
At a quarter to three?

New visions come to you,
Of things to forsake.
Is this called optimism,
Or something more fake?

'I'm going to stop drinking,'
'There'll be no more smoking,'
'Get a grip on my life,'
Just who are you joking.

Marcus Foreman

THEE BAG

My friend owned a tatty old bag,
not two or three but just thee bag,
she would want it wherever she went,
whether down to Devon or up to Kent,
always there just by her side,
it was even photographed with pride,
in it was absolutely everything,
matches, fags, and a teapot, what do you think,
in it all but the kitchen sink,
when it fell to pieces along the way,
she cried it cannot go it's got to stay,
she thought that it would be a sin,
to throw it out into the bin,
It carried on through day and night,
when the handle fell off it gave her a fright,
it was stitched and taped and had a patch,
her nerves were bad, no fags and no match,
The day arrived it had to go,
with cart outside and she did throw,
thee bag, someone shouted from far away,
this old bag has had its day,
gone forever, what a blow,
will she buy another,
           I don't know!

R Ellis

NOT MY KIND OF ART

In the press the other day
A student he sought with six heaps of hay
In the country the title, was supposed to portray
The asking price of this design of dried grass
Was the princely sum for £1000 cash
Was it pride In the effort foremost in mind
Or a get rich quick of a *heyday* kind?
Is it me that just can't consider it art
Am I old fashioned can't find in my heart
To see any beauty in this kind of art?
Another exhibit of an art display
Was a line of slates on the floor
Each slate overlapping needed patience for sure
Was it how to lay slates when doing a roof
To overlap them to make it rainproof?
As I stood surveying as to what it portrayed
I then read the title and just gazed and gazed
A five days climb of a mountain face?
Perhaps carrying the slates to put them in place
Was the inspiration of the effort he'd made
To guess what it was at a reasonable price
Would have made him more money than throwing a dice
It wasn't a mountain I saw with my eyes. It was
just a lost cause that some people call *art*

Ella Taylor

HAPPY FAMILIES

The children's laughter fills the air . . .
when coming out of school.
Yet, in the morn, the little dears
are downbeat, as a rule.

Their mothers, on the other hand,
sound cheerful as they go.
But on return, without a doubt,
the bonhomie is low.

And in the day, whilst they're away,
coffee mornings fit the bill . . .
where Jane and Joan and June extol
the virtues of the pill.

But when their other halves return,
there's a welcome . . . and a moan . . .
they'd have dusted more . . . and hoovered . . .
but for the bloody phone!

And in the evening, back together,
the mums make pots of tea . . .
and the dads go out for pizzas
and the children watch TV.

Afterwards, the romps till bedtime
bring the parents to their knees . . .
joys of laughter twinged with backache . . .
playing happy families!

Bryan Moore

HAIRY STORY
(Poem for Nathan)

I am Big Red the squirrel said
Not Ed or Fred give me some bread
And what's that on your head

The squirrel he did snatch the wig and threw it up a tree
The man he snarled and shook and stamped
The squirrel danced with glee

The cold assaulted his bald head he gave a mighty sneeze
The tree it shook the wig fell off and floated on the breeze

The strangest thing did happen then the way that strange things are
It took a swirl, a dip, a dance and fell into a car

The driver sat there all erect
And screamed into his mirror
It's not a thing that you'd expect
So rigid was his terror

'There must be something I have missed!' his voice was all a quake
With one flick of his shaking wrist he drove into the lake

The matted raft it floated off and finally came to rest
A huge great bird came from the sky and took it for a nest

The man he had to buy a hat to cover up his pate
He could not go out for a week the cruellest twist of fate

So when you're in the great outdoors you'd better have a care
And hold on to your precious wig
Lest squirrels steal your hair

Deborah Banks

THE OTHER SIDE OF CHRISTMAS

Someone has polished all the stars;
The moon has had a dusting, too.
Some busy hands have swept the clouds
And brushed the sky which looks like new.

What can this fuss be all about?
Why is there such activity?
A spring clean comes but once a year.
This is too much, it seems to me.

Down in the forest, so they say,
The firs and pines feel ill at ease.
They do not wish to be cut down
And then sold off as Christmas trees.

The holly bush is very cross;
Its temper shows in ruddy spots.
It does not want to lose its sprigs
Which will be put in plastic pots.

And nearby the mistletoe
Is blanching at the very thought
That secateurs will take their toll.
No wonder it looks overwrought!

One evening, as I sat alone,
Discordant music pained my ears.
Carol singers came to call -
The worst I'd heard for many years.

So this is what it's all about.
Now I know what I must do -
Throw my grumbles all away
And join the Yuletide ballyhoo.

Celia Georgina Thomas

POEM?

I can read a book,
when I sit a while.
I can make a funny look,
to coax a baby's smile.

I can cure a nettle sting,
when we are on a walk.
I can even dance and sing,
but it's better if I talk.

I can knit and sew,
to make a little square.
I can tie a ribbon bow,
to decorate your hair.

I can make and cook,
a pasty for my tea.
I can find a cosy nook,
with my plate upon my knee.

I am the only one I know,
to fall out of the bath.
To recite it blow by blow,
would surely make you laugh.

I can feel and think,
I can laugh and cry.
People push me to the brink,
can you tell my why?

I can talk with common man,
or with royalty converse.
I can tell a joke dead pan,
but I *cannot* write in verse.

Mary Elliott

WHITER THAN THE WHITEWASH ON THE WALL

As the lad was in Cheese Lane,
A small unmarked box fell off a lorry.
His father saw it was shaving sticks,
As soap was scarce, as good as lolly.
With the sticks mum washed the clothes,
Washed themselves all over, head to toe.
The lad had to wash behind his ears
Bringing vain protests and crocodile tears.
Washed all the dishes, any cleaning job
at all,
They were whiter than the whitewash
on the wall.

Ann Carey

MRS PERIVALE

I often heard the grown-ups talk of one
Whose conduct shocked and yet excited them;
Who did the things that simply were not done,
Like drinking gin in rooms reserved for men.

And other things half-heard and understood.
I did not need to see her. I just knew
That she was blonde and beautiful, with good
If too-bright clothes, and laughing eyes of blue.

And just too much, in fact a satiety
Of jewellery, expensive hat and veil.
She'd exude sex-appeal and gaiety,
This life-long 'friend' of Mr Perivale.

Time made her wife and widow in one day,
A gossips' topic whom I soon forgot.
We met at last, I viewed her with dismay.
Where were the furs, the hat, the bergamot?

The sex-appeal, the jewellery? I think
It was the gaiety I missed the most.
Perhaps her dowdy kindness was a link
For him with nanny, she could fill that post.

Barbara France

PRIVATE GLEE

On rare occasions, while zestfully disposed,
I bestow upon domestic air, a whistled tune.

With unemcumbered peace of mind,
My liberated spirit turns, in cheerful choice,
To this sweet shrill mix of lip blown notes

In preference to my singing voice.

But as seclusion so allows,

My various vocal ranges I rehearse,

So that imperfect, seldom practised repertoire
From arias, ballads, hymns and even scales

Is given even vent,
While as spouse on household chores
I am on faithful duty bent.

Now facile whistling seems less extrovert,

While singing brings courageous ego trips.

But gappy teeth leave whistling weak upon the lips

While tenor baritone or bass vibrate around the place
On short waves in the kitchen space.

Kith and kin grimace, while thankfully unseen,
As they endure my warbling on and on,
Until I clear my whistling singer's clean.

Perhaps forbearance to intrude upon my private glee,
Derives from understanding shrewd,

Of how euphoric vocalised washing up can be.

Clive Robson

SANTA'S NEW YEAR'S RESOLUTION

This year I'll cancel Christmas,
There'll be no first Noel:
And as for all my reindeer,
I'll cancel them as well.

This year I'll change the system
And move the festive feast
From Christmas back to Easter -
I am a rotten beast!

This year I'll fool those children
Who wait for me to call.
I won't come down their chimneys -
I'll not appear at all.

This year, there'll be no presents,
There'll be no mistletoe,
No holly and no ivy -
I'll even cancel snow.

This year, I'm only joking;
And you have got my leave
To hang up all your stockings
On this year's Christmas Eve

Brian M Wood

OLD KING COAL IS DEAD

Old King Coal was a filthy old soul
And a wicked old soul was he,
'Cos he crushed our young
And he choked their lung
And he killed full many a tree.

He ruled this land with a tyrant's hand
Though his subjects dreamed they were free.
They'd burrow and die
But believe the lie
'What a chosen bunch are we.'

They mourn the day that he passed away,
They can't believe that he's dead,
Yet this land is green
And never so clean
For we've chips and electronics instead.

Leonard Jarman

SMILE TO YAWN

Sitting in the fields with a smile,
Very chirpy was he,
Not a big smile I'd say,
Roughly about two foot three,

He stood up on the grass,
All four legs firmly on the ground,
Opened his big pair of lips,
And let out a moo-ing sound,

Up walks a big brown cow,
Very annoyed I'd say,
And with a very rough voice,
Says 'Is it games you like to play?'

Oh dear, not a very pleasant sight,
To say the least,
Let's just say,
Old smile had a very pleasant feast,

My little smile,
Was little no more
Instead he's a great big whopper,
Of six foot four,

Off trots he,
From dusk till dawn,
But now all he is,
Is a great big yarn,

So if you were to see old smiley,
Beware it's not time for dinner,
Co's this old smiley,
Just don't get any thinner.

Stuart Hooper

THE WEARY GARDENER

The grass need mowing and the fence needs painting,
Patio's cracked and the beans need staking,
The pond's sprung a leak and the fountain's not working,
Weeds are growing stronger while I get weaker,
Must be my age I'll take a breather.
Looks like the weather is going to get better,
I'll clean out the shed it's full of clutter and dig up that old tree stump
Already tripped over it and gone down with a thump,
Garden needs digging and seeds need sowing,
Sure will be a miracle if anything starts growing,
Hose pipe's old and perished just like me,
The Mrs is standing here and she quite agrees.
Wish I still smoked my dear old pipe,
But I got a bad heart and it gave me a fright,
My hair's gone grey and my sight is fading,
Soon won't tell the difference between cabbage and sprouting,
But I mustn't grumble I've had a good life,
'Cause always by my side has been my good lady wife.

Gillian L Glanville

PILES

We emerged one bright morning, the garden was
brown,
It wasn't the sun that had vanquished the
green,
Mountainous piles, spotted the lawn,
With bronze sticky pathways, winding between,
A sod perchance moved, just as we
inspected,
The tan tract 'tween fence and clothes
pole,
That's when we realised, we'd finally
detected -
The diarrhoea of Adrian the mole!

Thomas A Rattray

FEATS OF SPEED

The moon takes twenty eight days to glow,
There is always room for the river to flow,
The seasons come and go,
Faster than my toe-nails grow.

Rachel Lane

WHILE I AM HERE DOCTOR

Doctor, doctor, please help me.
First of all, my toes you see.
A hopeless case, I hear you say.
Shall we leave it for another day?

If toe problems were only one,
You might say something could be done.
When the problems mount to five
I suppose I am lucky to be alive.

Now about the pills I take
The reason for my visit, for goodness sake,
I take the pills when my heart beats fast.
I think it was far worse in the past.

Some people think I cannot hear
Perhaps you would look in my ear.
Sorry, what's that you say
You think I had better go away.

Joan Francis

WHY GRIPE?

I wandered over the meadows one day,
simply to pass the time away;
A cuckoo was calling, a skylark was singing,
Far in the distance the church bells were ringing.
The air was filled with the bees lazy buzz,
I was thinking how perfect everything was;
Then I came down to earth with a thud and a splat
flat on my face in a flippin' cow-pat.
I stared to curse, but upon reflection,
I thought that it might even help my complexion;
We drink cows milk from out of its udder,
so why gripe at what comes from under its rudder?

Edna J King

SUPERMARKET SHOPPING

Shopping in Waitrose, pushing trolleys
Avoiding babies and people's brollies
Gazing at shelves with a jaundiced eye
Wondering what I came in to buy.

I travel the aisles, up and down again -
I only came in to get out of the rain
Spoilt for choice, what shall I choose
Should it be cornflakes or bottles of booze?

Delicatessen? Paté or ham?
Do I need a pot of strawberry jam?
Shall I buy cod or a gleaming trout?
I don't know, I just wander about.

Ah, here are the offers - some half price -
Those chocolate biscuits look rather nice!
Are they a bargain? Hard to tell -
Wonder why they didn't sell?

There's Euro-sausage and Euro-cheese
And Euro-honey from Euro-bees.
I don't really fancy all that stuff
British food is good enough.

How about All-Bran to give me bounce?
And strange foreign fruit I can't pronounce?
Lemons are fresh - in a pretty pack -
I pick them up then put them back.

My trolley is empty - decidedly sparse -
The whole expedition is rather a farce.
I don't want anything, expensive or cheap -
I'll nip back home for an afternoon sleep.

One thing I must do - buy a packet of tea-
Then I'll get an hour in the car park - free!

Sybil Steel

THE DAY BRADLEY GLOBB TURNED INTO A BIRD

Such a grand and exuberant commotion occurred
The day Bradley Globb
Turned into a bird
The sprouting of feathers and protuberance of beak
Caused many a profanity
Of which I daren't speak

His father, despite an immaculate demeanour
Revolved round his tongue
Prose that could have been cleaner
His mother, endeared with a glorious refrain
Fainted however
Showing glorious disdain

The doctor was summoned to provide some review
Of this curious case
Causing such a to-do
But careful appraisal from beak down to tail
Could not find the root
Of this perplexing ail

The vicar, despite all deferential conviction
Piously failed
To revert the affliction
No manner of prayers or loud exorcising chants
Could prevent feathered filling
Of poor Bradley's pants

This dramatic transition from a boy to a bird
Was considered quite dreadful
And terribly absurd
But with consolation poor Bradley did squirm
It could have been worse
He could be a worm

David Harrison

P's C's And Me

I'm persistent persuasive provocatively nice
a rich taste of orient, filled with spice
I'm caring concerning creatively bright
a real little gem, shining at night

I'm patient placid possibly a pain
so much love to give, to all who want to gain
Compassion commitment to one particular crime
guilty in the first degree, innocence of time

I'm polite predictable presumably kind
a truly genuine person, seek and you will find
I'm captious calming completely alive
the little honey-pot, of bees to their hive

P's C's and me
Poppy cock! You see.

Linda Shropshire

Thoughts Of A Mature Student On Graduating From Anglia Polytechnic University

A college, a poly
upgraded by now
to university status
and how to remember her best
is a thought that concerns
those students whose lives she connected
made hell, made heaven
with fail or first
as each essay
devoured and digested
with comments divulged
how divergent our thoughts from teaching or tutor.

But, ready to leave
my thoughts more mature
perceive a problem
of which I'm unsure
was this late marriage of me and mind
arranged for better or worse?
Is gratitude due to matchmaker poly
as Anglia's campus I quit
or, at my age
shall I now find
though the brain has accepted the body's declined!

Christine Kilbee

THE TOMBOY

Mum was so delighted when she had a little girl;
Bows and pretty dresses - petticoats as well.
My thoughts were quite different it weren't really me!
I'd much prefer to swing on ropes, clamber up walls and trees;
play cowboys and Indians - didn't matter which.
My Grandma was disgusted . . . what would your mother think?
Prams and pretty dollies were changed for guns and tanks;
Home-made bows and arrows and other childish pranks.
I dreamed of knights, castles - battles won and lost;
perhaps I could be a boy . . . I might be better off -
or just another childish whim - part of growing up.

Eileen Gingell

THE MAN FROM PERU

From the top floor window he flew
The daring man from Peru.
Several somersaults in flight
He performed to excite.
His final dive set
Towards a missing safety net.

But quick as a flash
He turned, rolled, stumbled and crashed
To land unharmed in the street
His amazing act now complete.
To spontaneous applause and shouts of bravo what pluck
He bowed; before disappearing beneath an on coming truck.

Colin Farmer

WRITTLE WINE . . . NECTAR OF THE GODS

Writtle college wine is fine,
But you must drink it quick,
Because it tastes so 'orrible,
That it will make you sick.

The grapes they make this wine from,
Are picked when they're mature
And you can tell, by the bouquet,
They're grown in pig's manure.

It'll give you spots, it'll rot your socks,
It'll make your hair turn grey,
Or, if it's grey already,
It'll turn it back the other way.

It removes all stains, cleans out blocked drains,
It'll even clean out you,
When you've been to the curry house
And had a vindaloo.

It'll make rottweilers turn and run,
Don't give it to your cat,
They say its ozone friendly,
But I wouldn't bet on that.

It'll banish creepy-crawlies,
Deter the campus pest,
When he's knocking on your door at night,
Dressed only in his vest.

So, if your project's going wrong,
You seem to get nowhere,
Drink a glass of Writtle wine,
From then on you won't care.

David Kellard

THE ANTIQUES BODY SHOW

So often we see Antiques valued with some human adulation
What if there were experts of human valuation

Though Grandad's legs are bowed and thin and cannot run a mile
They may symbolise a certain age and a certain style

And Auntie Edna's ample chest with a certain graceful bow
Would certainly be so admired and judged the best in show

Young Susan with her fine young frame like a wine glass stem
Many dedicated collectors would like to get their hands round them

Cousin John and his bulbous trunk it bellied out in style
To get it to its beery best has taken quite a while

They'll never be collectors items no experts for to seek
Whatever their peculiarities they will always be unique

T Napper

LAUGH ALL THE WAY

To everyone sorrow comes
When they often feel low
But one need not look glum
'Laugh' as nature heals slow

Think of something cheery
And you will surely find
When thine day seems weary
You'll feel yourself unwind

A lesson to learn
Listen to the bird sing
Hence looking for his worm
As he flies on the wing

To laugh keeps ill away
And is a way of healing
Like the bird each day
Look around see life brimming

Having a good laugh
Is a way of relaxing
And to have a 'chaff'
Frees one from all sting

When the sun is shining
Everything seems brighter
If you laugh and keep smiling
Your heart will feel lighter

So when you feel down
Seek yourself a better day
Don't wear a frown
Just laugh all the way

Josephine Foreman

THOUGHT

I paused for thought did I
What thought occurred in my mind
I thought I was thinking
A problem ere long
The thought soon past
Methinks I was wrong

I paused for thought once again
What thought congealed in my brain
I thought of the last thought
But in my digress
I'd forgotten the present thought
That's what comes of thinking

Michael Gardner

WHERE IS YOUR HANKY DEAR?

A bit of string a copper ring
Two sticky Polo mints
One round pebble and something
Resembling a dragon (made of plastic of course) covered in fluff
A pink jelly baby a coin
(Five pence not quite enough to buy anything)
A smooth brown conker found probably in the park
A card from PG Tips collection
Depicting a white shark
A key-ring that answers to a whistle
(What a treasure) and a special toy
A red dinky car (Oh the things you find in the pocket of a small boy
Who just started school) But no handkerchief
Where is your hanky dear?

Daniela M Davey

THE GRAVEYARD

Walking alone
Looking around
Hoping, praying
To the silent ground.
The sound of feet
Makes your heart skip a beat.
As you look at the wall
You see nothing at all.
The clock strikes twelve
And the wind starts to blow
And all of a sudden
You think I've got to go.
But your plans
Are not taken into account
By the surrounding bodies
Who won't let you out.
You want to scream
You want to run
But there is no escape
You look around for an open gate.
You start to panic
Where can you go?
Just then
A friendly face appears
You're so glad to see them
You can't hide the tears.
But as you look
Deep into their eyes
You realise
They're not what they seem
All you can do is let out a scream!
You open your eyes and to your surprise
It was all just a dream.

Danni Turner

TRUTH IN JEST!

A film cartoon says it all
With a weird, way-out view
Of men and their affairs
And in technicolour too
All for amusement it seems
Yet, with each whacky lot
Is something serious
Existing behind the plot
An eye that always sees much
And understands so well
Film caricaturing
Of man's particular hell
      Giggling at pixies and elves
      Aren't we laughing at ourselves?

W T Martin

IRONING WITH DAMON

I always do my ironing
When Damon's on TV
How much ironing gets done
Depends on the Grand Prix
If Damon's driving well
And everything is fine
My shirt sleeves are perfection
My creases right on line
But if he's having problems
Any whisper of defeat
I'm afraid my folded clothes
Do not end up so neat
I love to watch each Grand Prix
My husband says that he can tell
By looking at his ironed shirts
If Damon Hill has driven well
I can't sit still for two whole hours
It's too much time to waste
And so I do my ironing
Watching Damon win his race!

Gill Morgan

SMILES

I give my help to all I can,
Each and every day.
Sometimes a smile is all I need,
To help me on my way,

If we all did a smile a day,
We'd travel very far,
You don't get them by the gallon,
You don't need a car,

All you need is a bubble,
Some happiness no doubt,
And when the bubble starts to burst,
Your smile comes pouring out,

You can get miles and miles of smiles,
But not very far on a frown,
I'd rather go far on a smile,
When I'm travelling into town,

You'll find that smiles are catching,
Like chicken-pox measles or mumps,
You just try smiling a little,
It's better than down in the dumps.

E Ensor

THE GOSLING

He was a gosling, fluffy and brown
His beak was big, his feathers still down.
How he wished his feet were smaller
His song was sweeter and his body taller.

He watched a lark as she skywards soared.
'If I could do that I'd never be bored.'
'I'd fly in the sky and sing like the lark'
'I'd sing and fly from dawn until dark.'

Just then from the reeds swam a gosling lady,
With a gentle quack reached the shallows shady.
Forgotten was the lark and his song so sweet,
Our hero swam with his lovely big feet.

Never again did he wish to embark
On an exchange trip with a sweet voiced lark.

D Dewhirst

DOING WHAT COMES NATURALLY

There are frogs in my garden, what a joy to behold
They are cuddling and loving no matter how cold,
They don't care who sees them they just carry on,
They will work overtime until the job's done.

The pond's full of spawn it's like something from space,
Even though you bend low you still can't see your face,
The water is churning like a storm out at sea,
Oh, I wish I could watch but I've got to get tea.

I've brought my tea with me to sit and take note
The kids have just called me a silly old goat,
I'm just so thrilled frogs have such a good time
It could give some ideas to this old man of mine.

M Horgan

AN OPTIMISTIC FUNGI

I am a little mushroom,
I grew up overnight
On a mushroom farm in Woking,
It's not a pretty sight.
But, I won't be here for very long.
A mushroom's life is short,
They wait until your're in your prime
And then cut off your stalk.
I don't know where I'll go from here
It depends on my condition,
But, if I'm firm and blemish free
I'll get instant recognition.
They'll pop me in a prepack
And send me to the shops,
Where a pretty girl will purchase me
To go with her pork chops.
So, if you're feeling down at heart
Dejected and forlorn,
Just think, you could have been like me
Up to your neck in spawn.
Not knowing of your destiny
Or what the future holds in store.
Ah! to be served up with fillet steak
I couldn't ask for more.
So be kind to all the mushrooms,
Remember, they have feelings too!
They go through life with big ideas
Then end up in a stew.

Irene Davies

SONG OF SABRE-TOOTHED TIGER

(Tune 'Clementine')

In a cavern, in a canyon,
   In the early Pliocene,
Lived a tiger, from the Niger,
And his sabre-toothy queen.
'O my Tusky, till I'm husky,
Will I praise your feline grace,
Herbivore, a plethora, will galumph about the place'.
Slew a mammoth, hairy mammoth,
Did that tusky, husky pair,
Without a cruet, they got through it.
Mammoth meal, for him and her!

Charles Bartlett

ATTRACTIONS

It started as a love affair
And lasted for awhile,
I fell for all your rounded shape
Admiring your distinctive style

I held you close and uttered words
You accepted what I said,
Persistently I held your frame
Then took you to my bed

As time progressed obsession grew
Your buttons thrilled me through,
Continually I had to talk
Unsure what else to do

I contemplated what was best
You absorbed my life complete
I needed you so much my dear
You swept me off my feet

But finally I made a choice
To leave you there alone,
I'm sorry, but it had to be,
My 'hungry *mobile-phone*'

Sam Royce

LAUGHTER THE BEST MEDICINE

It's in
Its shadow crossed my sight
My trembling limbs betray my fright.
My heart is pounding in my chest,
I think I'm running out of breath.
I must get out, I must escape,
I must decide which route to take.
I hear it moving closer now,
I must get out, I must, but how?

Just when I think I've had my chances,
And now must face the consequences,
A key is turned, the door flung wide,
My gallant knight is by my side.
With just a rolled up paper lance,
He sees my plight and takes a stance.
With just one blow then victorious shout
My nightmare fiend, the moth
Is out.

Pauline Stocks

DISBELIEF

How I love the politicians
On my television screen,
Who seem to think the public
Are absolutely green.

Who never answer questions,
Who argue black is white,
Think everybody else is wrong
While they alone are right.

Who vote themselves a large increase
When salaries are reviewed.
To be paid out immediately
While others sit and brood.

And doctors, nurses and the like,
Regarding their emoluments,
Are given about three per cent
In long drawn-out instalments.

And that, they tell us, is quite fair,
And maybe I am dense,
But I confess to me it doesn't
Make a lot of sense.

They tell us the economy
Is absolutely tops,
But would they think so if compelled
To buy from Oxfam shops?

And if they had to spend their nights
Sleeping in a box,
Or work for a couple of quid an hour?
I fancy they would not.

So of their flights of fancy
Would someone could relieve them,
And ask another question -
Do they think that we believe them?

John Taylor

OUR MILKIE

In wind and rain our pintas come,
The milk float at full throttle!
It's plain to see our milkman has,
Gotta lotta bottle!

Marjorie Chapman

ADVENTURE PLEASE

I'd like to feel again the joy
Of being six years old.
To dive into candyfloss
And lick ice-cream so cold.

At ten I'd explore river banks
And try to get my way.
I'd wheedle to stay up late,
Wondering, why is Gran's hair grey?

What happened to the urgent bliss
Of walking hand in hand?
It vanished after that first kiss,
Though more, of course, was banned.

The memory of the intense love
The babies' births engender
Will live forever in my heart -
Life's greatest adventure ever.

But what now? I often stop to ask,
My life span nearly done.
One more adventure if you please,
Before they lower me down.

Roma Scrivener

THE MOTORBIKE FROM HELL

For all the years that I've loved you
That demon's ruled your life
Such devotion to its welfare
Has caused me inner strife!

I know I have been second best,
In spite of all you've said,
You dashed back home to dip its chrome
The day that we were wed.

By the kissing gate on our first real date
Beneath the summer stars,
You said you loved me so,
But you had to go,
To align your handlebars!

I've never known what it is to own
A man who is neat and clean,
You are soused in oil, and our chairs you spoil
When you stain them black and green.

When you and Will and cousin Phil
Meet up at a family wake,
The talk soon turns to 'ports' and 'burns',
And what speed that beast should make.

When Christmas comes and the deep frost numbs,
All kneeling on the floor,
Hell's Angels and their leathered friends
Have journeyed to adore.

'That bike of mine has become a shrine!'
Your friends you often tell,
I love you still, but I wish 'it' ill,
the 'motorbike from Hell'.

Betty Duberley

WHAT A MESS

Oh dear, I've done this twice in a week
I've stepped in a mess and now I stink.
I know it was very dark at the time
Mind you, that's no fault of mine.

When back home I did arrive,
I had to clean these boots of mine.
It wasn't a job I was in favour of
'Cos when I had finished I didn't 'arf pong.

So into the bath I had to go.
For to wash myself from head to toe.
Now all I can say is don't do it again
Otherwise I might wash myself completely away.

Rosetta Smith

OUR MOLLY

I have a younger sister who is naughty as can be.
Now I'm a little angel, she is not at all like me.
We are going to get evicted, 'cause of the neighbours, they complain,
Especially her in 28 - we think she is nothing but a pain.

It was our Molly's birthday so we thought what could we do?
Finishing school at half-past three we went off to the zoo.
The lions looked so miserable our Molly had to let them out,
The keeper he was so annoyed - you should have heard him shout!

After this we caught the bus and got off at the pier.
Across the road lives Auntie Jill - thought we'd call to see her
But Auntie she is never in - she was shopping in the town.
Her nice clean washing on the line, guess who pulled it down?

The Queen came to our town last week - she did a walkabout.
Red carpet lay regal and proud - of that there was no doubt.
When she came back to her car - smiles turned into a frown,
Her gaze resting on two front tyres, someone had just let down!

Now security it acted real fast and the army was called in.
What our Molly had now done, it sure was her biggest sin.
But I still love my sister even though she treats me bad,
I go to visit her in jail. Don't you think that's sad?

John Bland

CHILDISH CONFUSION

My dad wears an earring, well I think he is my dad,
He also has long blonde hair just like my mum once had.
Around his neck hang lots of chains, you can see him from afar
And when the sun shines on him he glitters like a star.
Rings adorn all fingers as well as both his thumbs
And they must all have cost a lot, they're better than my mum's.
On one wrist he wears bracelet with his name for all to see
On the other is a big gold watch almost as big as me.
He also has his hair done, cut, shampooed and set
And once he went and had it permed, my mates are laughing yet.
I know that he wears trousers but then so does my mum
And when he comes out the bathroom, cor he don't half hum.
He smells a lot like Auntie Pat, who wears the smartest clothes,
She's the one with the long fur coat, yeah, he's got one of those.
Perhaps you think I worry, too much for just a lad,
But have I really got two mums or is one of them my dad?

Ken Woodmason

CAW

Early morning travellers, bouncing along as if to work
Not in any particular hurry, even have time to talk.

Flapping and cawing together, in a disorganised jovial group.
Left their tree homes behind, like chickens away from the coop.

This field or that, they may settle, have a glean like clients in a shop.
Follow the plough for an hour or two, then on to the next feeding stop.

They return home in the evening, in similar style through the sky.
The weather determines their speed, but the rooks fly on, low or high.

Jenny Major

FIRST LOVE

My first love gave me a rose
At school on that first day
And thrusting it beneath my nose
I thought I heard him say
I love you more than anyone
I've ever loved before
But I didn't buy this rose for you
I pinched it from next door.
That flower meant the world to me
The first I'd ever had
And though the lad had pinched it
It really made me glad
That he could think so much of me
That he got for me a flower
I loved him more than anything
And more so by the hour.
The very next day at school
I let him lick my lolly
And then I watched in horror
As he gave a rose to my friend Polly

Jacqui Jones

THE DUSTER'S LAMENT

Why do I always have to be yellow
Why can't I be white like my silver cloth fellow?
I'm not afraid of a bit of grey dust
To colour me yellow, I think is unjust
I could maybe be red or a rich shade of brown
Even the floor-cloth treats me with a frown
He's grey, with a border of heavenly blue
To treat me as cowardly just will not do
Next time you go shopping, just ponder and think
And look for a duster in bright shocking pink.

Cathie Bridger

INSANE POETRY

I f you could live your life again
N ot that puberty bit (that would be insane)
S ay, what would you like to be?
A sculptor, a painter or an extraordinary tree
N ever mind the tree bit let me be a slug
E very leaf there'd be slime, every twig I'd tug

P erhaps I'm crazy or maybe insane
O mitting my mind and life to a solitary name
E veryhere I'd go I'd leave a trail of slime
T o claim every tread of life for 5 minutes 'mine'
R emember, it's only imagination, it's only a game
Y et I'm not crazy, for I'm a poet by name!

Rebecca Rosenthal

NEW COAT WANTED

Winnie the bulldog had lost her hair
Giving rise to many a joke.
This was remedied quickly
By getting her a coat.

We walked to the park one day
The weather was cold and freezing.
But at least with her posh new coat on
We didn't get any teasing.

Halfway round, we came to the pond.
A thin layer of ice on the top.
Winnie trotted over a bit too far
And in she went with a plop!

She paddled away in a panic
This being her first time swim.
Close to the edge we grabbed her collar
Hoping *we* wouldn't fall in.

Hauling her out was no mean task
She's a sturdy dog, you could say.
Her coat came off in a jiffy
She shivered on this ice cold day.

We hurried home as quick as we could.
Well, as quick as Winnie could be.
We didn't want to meet anyone
'Cos I'm afraid she looked like ET!

Jennifer Batson

WRIST IN PIECES

(Dedicated to Big Johnathan Fitzgerald)

Let me tell you the tale of a good friend of mine, a young lad,
                                        BJ is his name.
He rode off one day on his trusty pushbike, delivering the papers
                                        his game.
All that he did, he did with a will, so he pedalled round Maltby
                                        at speed,
All of his papers delivered on time and his customers - happy indeed.

Early one morn to the shop he did ride, bade a hearty good morning
                                        to Andy.
Loaded his bag with papers galore, four Beanos, two Puzzlers and
                                        a Dandy.
Thus laden down he climbed on his bike and set off on his forty
                                        mile round
Delivering papers with a grin and a wave, and all this for just less
                                        than a pound!

At the first fifty houses all was OK he delivered the papers
                                        right proper.
But as he came down the hill he pulled on his brakes and BJ he came
                                        a right cropper.
When he pulled on the brakes it made the bike stop, in fact it worked
                                        like a charm.
But though the bike stopped, poor BJ did not and he hit the floor
                                        with his arm.

As he lay on the ground in considerable pain, he hoped someone
                                        would assist.
He'd grazes and bruises and multiple aches and what's more, a slight
                                        broken wrist.
His elbow swelled up just like a balloon, a crack in the bone was
                                        the cause,
So he stood and he bled with an ache in his head, and he looked at
                                        his bike in remorse.

He knew he was hurt and needed first aid and he knew where to go
for assistance.
So he staggered around to Rolling Dales Close and knocked on
the door with persistence.
So they dialled 999 and shouted for help and an ambulance was
soon on the spot.
They plastered him up from his head to his foot, poor BJ had all gone
to pot.

Chris Lawery

THE FLATULENT MARE

I am a London Cabby
And my mare's a lovely lass
But, poor old gal's turned flatulent
I'll turn her out to grass.
Why just this very morning
I could hardly hide my face
I was really quite embarrassed when
She dropped one in front of Her Grace.

I'd just picked up the duchess
Who was off to launch a ship
I was bowing really courteously
When the old mare, she lets rip
I apologise most humbly
For her hearing something so coarse
She says 'Actually Battersby I thought it was the horse.'

David Morley

MY LIVING ROOM DOORWAY

my living room doorway
it's a funny place to be
it should be more to the left
'mm' maybe to the right
all it ever does is stand there and tease

I have never been happy with it
now even more so
my mind says it shouldn't be there
so I cuff it with my toes

now the final anguish
whilst in a hurry I broke my toe
dam the doorway ban it from the house
still I'd better not
what else would fill that slot

Gabby Copperstone

THE DREAM

Last night I dreamed I was a bird
With wings so strong and broad
And up into the universe
I flew and swooped and soared.
I came upon the fluffy clouds
As soft as cotton wool
And saw in them reflected
The beauty of the soul.
Oh, it was simply wonderful
To be so near to heaven.
I felt that all my earthly sins
Could readily be forgiven.
I flew into a sunset of beautiful radiant hue
Where orange, red and golden lights
Faded into a distant blue.
And then I felt the raindrops
And saw the rainbow arc
And knew I had to find the end
That dropped into the park.
Down I fell - just like a stone
And landed as if I were dead
And when I awoke with a sudden start
I'd fallen out of bed!

Joan E Picken

IT'S GOOD FOR YOU

Don't play golf, tomorrow
You won't, have time.
And don't do that job
You said, you'd do mine.
You can't do this
You can't do that
And you must, start slimming
You're getting too fat.
You must stop smoking,
It's bad for me.
And stop taking sugar in your tea.
Yes, everyone's telling me how to be.
Others deciding what's best for me.
Outsiders, minding my business, and yours.
They're a pain in the neck, and depressive bores.
Royal jelly, garlic pills, unsaturated fats.
Take all this health food.
Then catch asthma from cats.
I live in a democracy.
I'm supposed to be free.
Surely I can decide, what's good for me.
Or can I?

John Maguire

MY SHADOW

Silently slithering over the ground,
Jumping and sliding it goes,
Following me everywhere I may go,
It appears it's attached to my toes.

Whenever the weather is cloudy or dull
My shadow it leaves me in peace,
But out comes the sun to give it more strength
Then my privacy again it will cease.

Jumping and weaving, climbing and sliding,
It will not come detached,
It seems to be guarding, perhaps it's my spirit,
Some game that the angels have hatched.

It's never in colour, it's always translucent,
It's a flatter invention of me,
At least I'm not lonely with my shadow connected,
Instead of just me it becomes we.

Pamela Cooper

THE THIEF OR BLACKBIRD

My gold rings were stolen
    by an oversized crow,
    or maybe a raven
    I really don't know.

I'd taken off my gold bands
    to wash up a plate,
Then down swooped that monster
    who was perched on the gate.

I knew that he pilfered
    and stole small things,
    but who would have thought
    he'd have taken my rings?

Now like Sherlock Holmes
    I look around
    to see if that thief
    has flown onto the ground.

To most folks the blackbird
    may appeal,
But do they know
    of its ability to steal?

Yvonne Bacon

OH DEAR

I look in the mirror, and what do I see?
Who is that old woman that looks back at me?
I step on the scales, and oh what a shock
No wonder the buttons won't meet on my frock
I bend down to fasten the lace in my shoe
And my face colours up to a bright scarlet hue
It doesn't seem long since I danced all night
No chance of it now, my shoes are too tight
I remember the waltzes, quicksteps and tango
But now it's an effort to get up and go
And get into line in the post-office queue
Where we 'old dears' draw the money that's due
Alas and alack, what else can I say?
'Cept, will I be here on my next birthday?

Joan Fletcher

THE CAT WOMAN

I once met a maiden,
Who was moggie mad,
'Feline fanatic'
She had it quite bad.

I'd paws for thought,
But to no avail.
She would only love you
If you had four legs, and a tail.

I tried to grow long whiskers,
And learnt how to purr,
But when it came to loving
The cat, was always there.

I changed my name to Tom,
What else could I do?
I even bought foundation,
Called Burmese Blue.

In the end I knew
This girl was not for me,
She took me to the vet,
And gave me Whiskas
For my tea.

Derrick Evers

A Visit To The Dentist

Off to the dentist I solemnly go
Nothing to it really you know
Having made the appointment sometime ago
The usual check-up, my teeth to show

Sit in the chair and open wide
Whilst the dentist takes a look inside
'What have we here?' he says with glee
'Some loose ones on the bottom row I see'

He asks me question, I give a sigh
With a mouthful, how do I reply?
'I want to splint these teeth together
They will last for a while but not forever

First the hygienist will work on you
Make your teeth sparkle and look like new
She works hard to clean away tartar and plaque
If I had my way I would give her the sack

It was at this time that I began to dread
Have I something wrong inside my head?
I go through all this hurt and pain
I feel brave and do not complain

The day arrived for the splint to take place
The dentist seemed to be working at a fast pace
Drying the mouth out, it looked like a prune
The splint took place, it was one day in June

There was no pain nor did I feel ill
The pain came later when paying the bill
So when you are taken over by fear and dread
Think of others who suffer more pain instead

Alan Thorley

THE GRUMBLIES

When it's late in the evening, and no-one's about
and Mummy is sleeping, the Grumblies come out.
Now, the Grumblies are horrid,
The Grumblies are mean,
the nastiest people you ever have seen.
Little and crooked with faces of green,
and the skinniest arms that you ever have seen!

They come in the kitchen and spill all your milk,
and tear your best dresses of satin and silk.
They run up your hallway and bang on your door,
and empty your rubbish all over the floor.
They write on wallpaper, they play in the loo,
and leave things untidy and blame it on you.
Then when you are sleepy and ready to doze,
they start you off sneezing by tweaking your nose!

But if you're a good girl and if you are nice,
they will fill up your dreams with brown sugar and spice.
They'll keep watch upon you when you go to bed,
and see you sleep safely and cuddle your ted.
They'll fill up your tea plates with ice-cream and jelly,
and so you keep smiling they'll tickle your belly.
For if there's one thing that the Grumblies despise,
it's to see just one tear in those great big brown eyes.
So be a good girl and be kind to your mum,
and while you are sleeping, the Grumblies will come!

A J Marchant

EVENTIDE

I know my face has seen better days
Battered by rain wind and the sun's rays
The deep lines remind me of Spaghetti Junction
But at 75 I'm lucky it's still able to function.

The old eyes that were once a brilliant blue
Has now become a very different kind of hue
They're glazed, need glasses, all yellow and red
Got that tired look as if I'm ready for bed.

The voice once strong and vibrant to hear
Is now just a croak and very unclear
Vowels and consonants just don't sound right
They sound all slurred just as if I'm tight.

The old body too is a bit of a shambles
Legs just won't go any faster than an amble
They just won't do what the old heart desires
I think someone up there is putting out the fire.

C W Semmens

SPACE SHOT

The Irish have entered the space race -
They're going to outdo all the rest
To prove that the Irish aren't stupid.
Their target? You'll never have guessed.

Not for them just the moon, or a planet -
No, *they're* going to land on the *sun*.
Cape Kennedy's anxious and worried,
And says it just cannot be done.

But the Irish have answered as follows:
'With confidence we'll make the flight.
Sure, we know it's too hot in the daytime -
So we'll land up there during the night.'

Paddy Ariss

MY HANDY HUSBAND

My husband likes to fix things, even though they are not broke,
But it keeps him happy, he's a cheery, smiley bloke.
I've bought him expensive presents, but these he did not like,
He'd rather have a box of nuts, or something for his bike.
So this year, for his birthday, I'll obey the golden rule,
And buy him something broken or a nice new handy tool.

Lara Higgins

GET YOUR KICKS AT AGE 66

Cookridge was a quiet place, relaxing and serene,
But now those days are long since gone, someone's blown
the calming scene.
For from the gates of No 1 comes a rider dressed in black,
Youth regained, born to ride, he ain't never going back.

You can see him on a clear day, the sun glinting off
the chrome,
(It must be clear, 'cos if it rains he's got to clean
it when he's home)
John Lyttle is that rider's name, to me it's just
plain Dad;
He's got a machine, black and mean; we all
thought that he was mad.

Fellows of a similar age wear flat caps and
play whist,
But John just tears off down the road with one
flick of his wrist.
So he'll cruise the dales of Yorkshire, his
two-fifty gives its all,
Recalling earlier biking years when his
brother broke his fall.

So, may the road rise up before you
And the wind be on your back
And as the Irish often put it
'Just enjoy the crack'.

Tim Lyttle

INFORMATION

We hope you have enjoyed reading this book - and that you will continue to enjoy it in the coming years.

If you like reading and writing poetry drop us a line, or give us a call, and we'll send you a free information pack.

Write to :-

Anchor Books Information
1-2 Wainman Road
Woodston
Peterborough
PE2 7BU